THOMAS JEFFERSON

By Linda Wade

Illustrated by
Karen Neulinger

© **1993 January Productions, Inc.** All rights reserved, including the right to reproduce the book or parts in any form.

Library of Congress Catalog Card No. 92-074521
Printed in the United States of America
ISBN 0-87386-084-5 (Paperback Edition)
ISBN 0-87386-885-3 (Library Edition)

THOMAS JEFFERSON

Thomas Jefferson was born on April 13, 1743. He was the first son of Peter and Jane Randolph Jefferson. Thomas and his two older sisters lived on a small plantation called Shadwell. Shadwell was in Albemarle County, in the western part of the Virginia Colony. Thomas could see the Blue Ridge Mountains in the distance as he played in the yard.

The Jeffersons were well liked and received many visitors. Few people lived in the western part of Virginia in those days. When visitors came, they usually stayed for a few days. Even the Indians, who distrusted most white men, stopped for visits with the Jeffersons. Thomas and his sisters learned a lot from them.

When Thomas was two years old, his parents became guardians of four children. The children's parents, Mr. and Mrs. William Randolph, had recently died. William Randolph was Mrs. Jefferson's cousin and a close friend of Mr. Jefferson. The Jefferson family moved to the Randolph estate, called Tuckahoe. This large estate on the James River was only a few miles from Richmond. Here their social life was very active! Thomas and his sisters learned a lot about social manners, dancing and other conventions of society. When Thomas was five, he joined the older children in the one-room schoolhouse on the estate. A private tutor taught them reading, writing and arithmetic.

When Thomas was nine, his family moved back to Shadwell. Mr. Jefferson hired a teacher for Thomas and his sisters. But Mr. Jefferson wanted Thomas to get a better education. So he arranged for him to go to a school near Tuckahoe. For the next five years, Thomas was tutored by the Reverend William Douglas. He learned French, Latin and Greek.

Even then it was easy to see that Thomas was very bright. And he was interested in so many things! He had a notebook that he took with him wherever he went. In it he wrote down the names of all the birds and animals he saw. He listed the details of the plants and insects, too.

Thomas's father was a part-time surveyor and spent a lot of time in the wilderness. Thomas often went with him. Mr. Jefferson showed him how to draw maps of the rivers and mountains. He talked to him about the great river that flowed to the Pacific Ocean. Thomas listened with fascination. These were happy times.

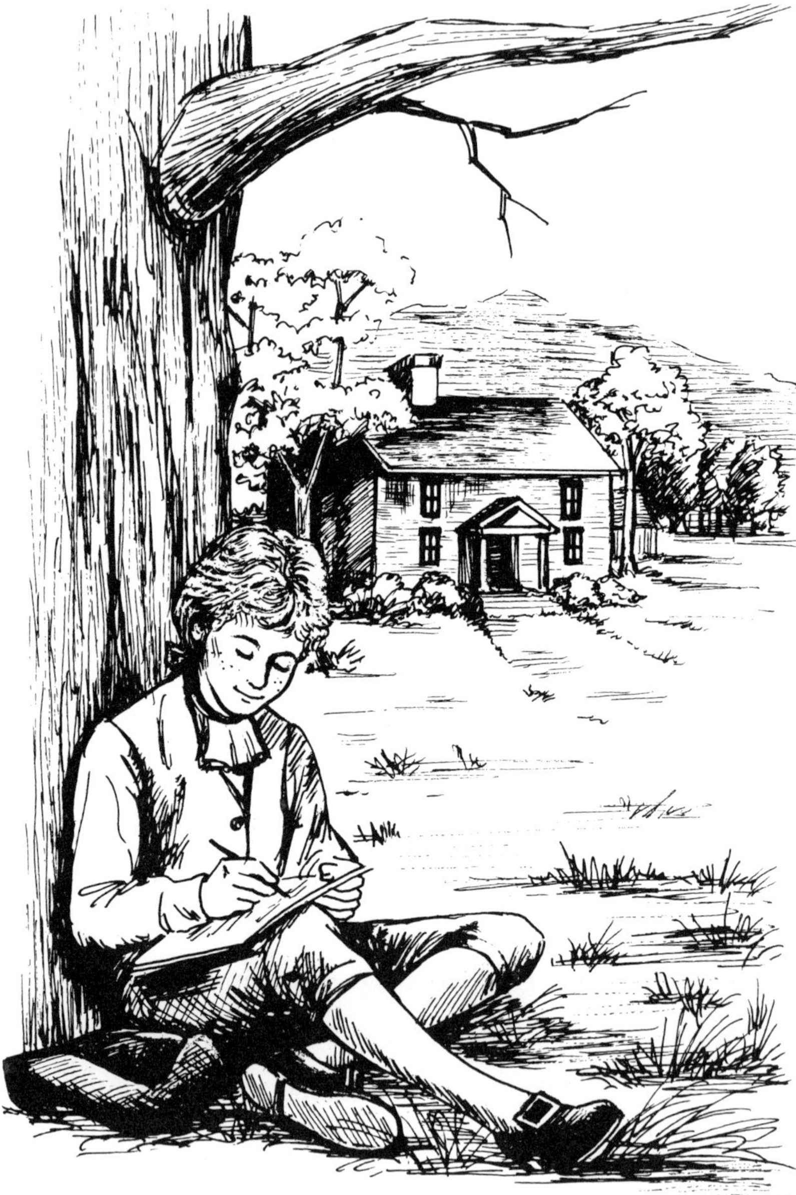

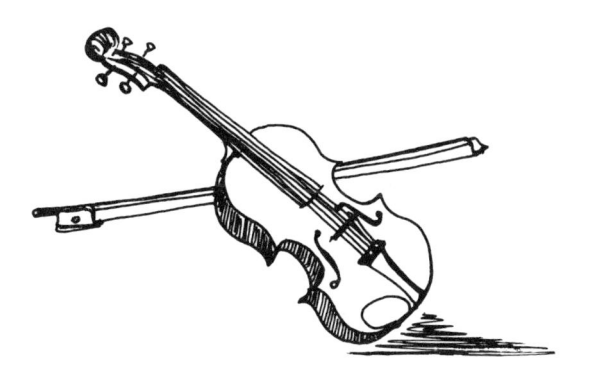

But when Thomas was fourteen, his world changed drastically! His father died. Mr. Jefferson had wanted his son to have a good education. So friends arranged for Thomas to go to a small school near Shadwell. The teacher was the Reverend James Maury. Thomas studied geology and botony as well as Latin, Greek and French. He loved learning about the plants and animals that had fascinated him for so long. He also began to read books about philosophy and government.

But his interests were not limited to what he learned in school. He was a skilled rider and learned to hunt. He also loved music and became an excellent violinist.

By sixteen, Thomas was ready for more advanced studies. The tall, red-headed young man said goodbye to his family and left for the College of William and Mary. It was in Williamsburg, at that time the capital of Virginia. Although there were only about 200 houses and 1,000 people, Williamsburg was the largest city Thomas had ever seen. It was very exciting!

While at William and Mary, Thomas met many interesting people. Some would have a great influence on his life. One such man was his professor Dr. William Small. Dr. Small introduced him to an attorney named George Wythe and to the governor of the colony, Francis Fauquier. These great men were very impressed by the young man from Albemarle. They often included him in their private gatherings. The foursome spent many evenings at the governor's mansion, talking and playing chamber music. Thomas felt honored to be included!

Thomas especially admired George Wythe—not only because he was a great attorney, but also because he had freed all of his slaves. Although Thomas hated slavery and was deeply disturbed by it, he never freed the slaves he inherited.

In 1762, when his studies at William and Mary were complete, Thomas began to study law under George Wythe. In 1767 Thomas took and passed the bar exams. He could have taken them sooner, but first he wanted to learn all he could. Before long, Thomas gained a reputation as a fine lawyer. He used most of his earnings to buy more books.

Like most well-educated landowners of the time, Jefferson entered politics. In 1768 he was elected to the Virginia legislature, called the House of Burgesses.

But the election was not all that was on his mind. Thomas had dreamed of having a home on the mountain behind Shadwell. He had fond memories of that mountain; he and his father had explored it together often.

Thomas had read many books on architecture and had become quite good at it. He planned and supervised the building of a beautiful new mansion. He called it Monticello, or "little mountain" in Italian. When a fire destroyed Shadwell in 1770, Thomas moved into the partially built house.

That same year Thomas met Martha Wayles Skelton. She was a twenty-year-old widow. The two saw each other often. On January 1, 1772, Thomas and Martha were married. Theirs would be a happy marriage. They would have one son and five daughters. Sadly, all but two would die in childhood.

Life in the colonies in those years was uncertain. The colonists were unhappy with the way in which England was taxing them. Talk of revolution spread.

In 1773 Jefferson helped organize a Committee of Correspondence in Virginia. These committees were set up to help the colonies unite against Britain. Patrick Henry and George Washington were also members of the Virginia committee.

In 1774 representatives were chosen to meet in Philadelphia for the First Continental Congress. Thomas was sick and could not attend, but he wrote his views and sent them to be read. He argued that the British Parliament had no control over the American colonies.

Jefferson did attend the Second Continental Congress in the spring of 1775. By this time some people were talking about breaking ties with England—about fighting for independence. Plans were made to form an army. George Washington was chosen to be Commander-in-Chief of the new Continental Army.

12

On June 7, 1776, Richard Henry Lee of Virginia presented a document to Congress. In it he proposed independence. John Adams of Massachusetts seconded it. No one knew if the proposal would pass. But if it did, they wanted to be prepared.

A committee was appointed to prepare a paper declaring independence. On the committee were Benjamin Franklin, John Adams, Roger Sherman and Robert Livingston. Everyone agreed that Jefferson was the best writer. He was chosen to write the draft.

Debate went on for days. Many did not want to break away from England. Some went home rather than sign. But on July 2 the resolution passed.

Two days later—on July 4, 1776—the document known as the Declaration of Independence was adopted. There had been few changes from Jefferson's original draft. However, a section in which he denounced slavery was not included. Few ideas in the declaration were new. But now they were written for all to see.

In September Jefferson resigned from Congress. He wanted to be with Martha. She had lost a baby and was not well.

Jefferson returned to the Virginia House of Delegates. From 1777 to 1779 he headed a committee to revise Virginia's laws. He was responsible for many important reforms:

Inheritances no longer had to go to the firstborn son. (This angered many aristocrats.)

The importation of slaves into Virginia was prohibited.

Separation of church and state in Virginia became law.

The laws of Virginia were rewritten to make them easier to understand.

The death penalty was abolished except for murder or treason.

There would be three years of free primary school for all children.

In 1779 the Virginia Assembly elected Thomas Jefferson the second governor of the state. Patrick Henry had been the first. Jefferson did not like being a war-time governor. He was frustrated by his inability to stop the British invasion of Virginia. When his two terms were over, there was an investigation about his actions. The results brought nothing but praise for Jefferson; he was even chosen to be a delegate to the Continental Congress. But Jefferson was hurt by the investigation. He resigned his seat in the Continental Congress and said he would never again hold a public office.

Back home at Monticello, Jefferson received many visitors. He was a man of many interests and could hold a conversation on just about any subject. Among his favorites were agriculture, law and philosophy, the classics, economics, and medicine.

Jefferson enjoyed his life at home. That is, until tragedy struck. In September 1782 Martha died. Jefferson became very depressed. He spent most of his time alone in his library. Finally, his ten-year-old daughter, Martha, nicknamed Patsy, coaxed him to go riding with her. Although he still grieved, he began to see his friends again. It was time to get on with his life.

In May 1784 Congress asked Jefferson to join John Adams and Benjamin Franklin, who were in France to negotiate treaties of commerce. Jefferson accepted. When Franklin resigned as Minister to France in 1785, Jefferson replaced him.

Jefferson had taken his oldest daughter, Martha, with him to France. In 1787, his daughter Polly joined them. Sadly, his youngest daughter, Lucy, died before they returned to America.

While in Europe, Jefferson did a lot of traveling. He took the opportunity to learn all he could. He was especially interested in learning more about architecture and methods of farming.

Of course, he also kept informed about events back home. He knew about the 1787 Constitutional Convention. He was glad that George Washington had been chosen President. But he was upset that the Constitution did not contain a bill of rights.

Thomas and his two daughters left for America in October 1789. Although he loved France, he was anxious to return to Monticello. On the way home, they stopped at his sister's home. Awaiting him was a letter from President George Washington. "Will you come to be secretary of state?" the letter said. Jefferson was surprised. He would have preferred to remain at Monticello.

He discussed Washington's offer with his close friend James Madison. Madison had studied law under Jefferson. Now, however, it was Madison's turn to give Jefferson advice. He urged him to accept the offer. Jefferson reluctantly agreed. He left his daughters in his sister's care and headed for the capital in New York. On the way, he stopped to visit his dying friend, Benjamin Franklin.

As secretary of state, Jefferson had many disagreements with Alexander Hamilton, secretary of the treasury. As time went on, the division between them grew worse. Political differences between the two men led to the development of the first political parties in America. The Federalists adopted Hamilton's principles. They favored a strong central government run by the rich. They also favored a national bank.

Jefferson's followers became known as the Democratic-Republicans. Although often called Republicans, they were closer in their beliefs to modern-day Democrats. They believed in states' rights and the strict interpretation of the Constitution. They also believed that the common people should be given more power in the government. The Republicans got most of their support from the small farmers, the frontier settlers and the northern laborers.

On December 31, 1793, Jefferson resigned as secretary of state and returned to Monticello. He was determined to concentrate on his estate and to get things back in order. He worked out a design for a new plow. He started a nailery on the estate. He also established a cabinetmaker's shop, a carpenter's shop and a bricklayer's yard. Jefferson neither wanted nor expected to hold another public office.

Once again Jefferson's expectations were wrong. In 1796 Washington announced that he would not run for a third term. Jefferson became a presidential candidate without even expressing an interest in running. Madison and his other followers did most of the campaigning.

At that time the candidate with the most votes became President. The runner-up became vice president. John Adams, who had 71 electoral votes, won the election. He was sworn in as President in Philadelphia, now the capital of the United States. Thomas Jefferson, with 68 electoral votes, was sworn in as vice president. Adams was a Federalist. Jefferson was a Republican. Although Jefferson and Adams had been close friends, by the end of Adams' term their friendship had ended.

In 1800 Jefferson ran against Adams for the presidency. This time he launched an active campaign. Among the issues in his campaign were the Alien and Sedition Acts. The Alien Act said the President could exile anyone thought to be dangerous to the United States. The Sedition Act made it possible to jail people for criticizing the federal government. Jefferson believed that these acts, passed during Adams' term, went against the first amendment of the Constitution!

Thomas Jefferson received 73 votes. So did Aaron Burr, whom the Federalists had intended to be Jefferson's vice president. The election was to be decided by the House of Representatives. After 36 ballots, Thomas Jefferson was elected President of the United States. In 1804 the law would be changed so that the President and vice president would run on the same ticket.

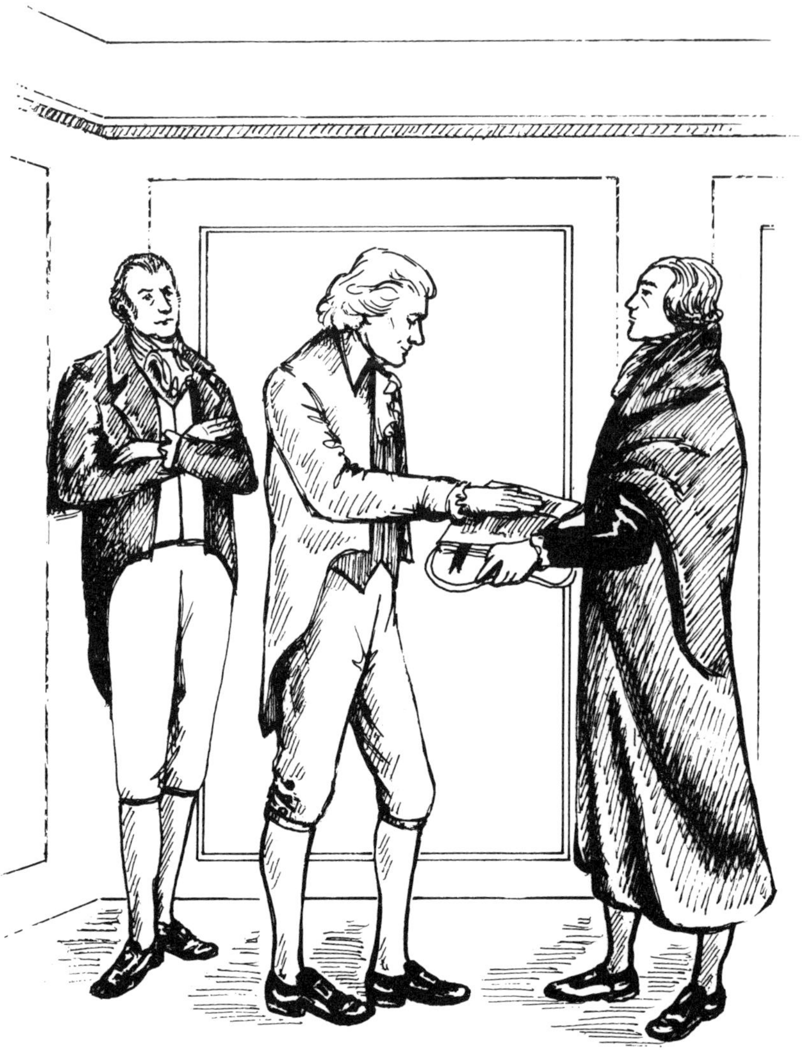

The President's House—now called the White House—in the newly founded capital of Washington, was only partly built when Jefferson moved in. Jefferson wanted to pull the country together. In his inauguration speech he told the people, "We are all Republicans. We are all Federalists."

Jefferson appointed his friend James Madison secretary of state. Madison's wife Dolley often served as first lady. This honor was shared with Jefferson's daughter Martha.

The most important event of Jefferson's first term was the purchase of the Louisiana Territory. This region had belonged to France and then to Spain. In 1802 Jefferson learned that Spain had ceded the area back to France. He got two million dollars from Congress. Then he instructed Robert Livingston and James Monroe to negotiate for the purchase of New Orleans, which was part of the territory.

To Jefferson's surprise, Napoleon, the Emperor of France, decided to sell the entire territory for about fifteen million dollars! In 1803 the size of the United States doubled!

Jefferson thought back to his childhood. He remembered the stories his father had told him about the river that went to the great ocean. He wanted to know more about the western lands.

An exploration party was formed. It was to be headed by Meriwether Lewis and William Clark. They were to survey the vast lands that had been added to the United States. The expedition went to the headwaters of the Mississippi. It crossed the Rocky Mountains and went all the way to the Pacific Ocean. They brought back detailed records of what they saw. No longer were these western lands a mystery!

Thomas Jefferson's first term ended in public glory but private grief. His daughter Polly died after giving birth to her second child. Of his six children, only Martha still lived.

Jefferson easily won a second term. By this time, however, war had broken out between Great Britain and France. Jefferson was determined to keep the United States out of the war, but it wouldn't be easy.

The British had been stopping and searching American merchant ships for British deserters. It was difficult to tell the Americans from the British. Many American seamen were forced into the British navy. To make matters worse, the French said they would seize any ship that allowed itself to be boarded by the British!

In 1807 the British frigate *Leopard* attacked the U.S. frigate *Chesapeake* when the captain refused to allow his ship to be searched. Jefferson expelled British warships from American waters. The British cabinet expressed regret about the *Chesapeake* incident. But it would not agree to stop searching American ships for deserters.

Jefferson knew the United States was not prepared for war. Instead, he asked Congress to pass an embargo bill. The Embargo Act of 1807 prohibited American ships from leaving the United States for any foreign port. It was difficult to enforce. Smuggling flourished.

But American trade suffered badly. The New England merchants were the first to demand repeal of the embargo. Unemployed farmers, sailors and shipbuilders joined them. Finally, Jefferson reluctantly gave in. On March 1, 1809—just three days before Jefferson left office—Congress repealed the Embargo Act.

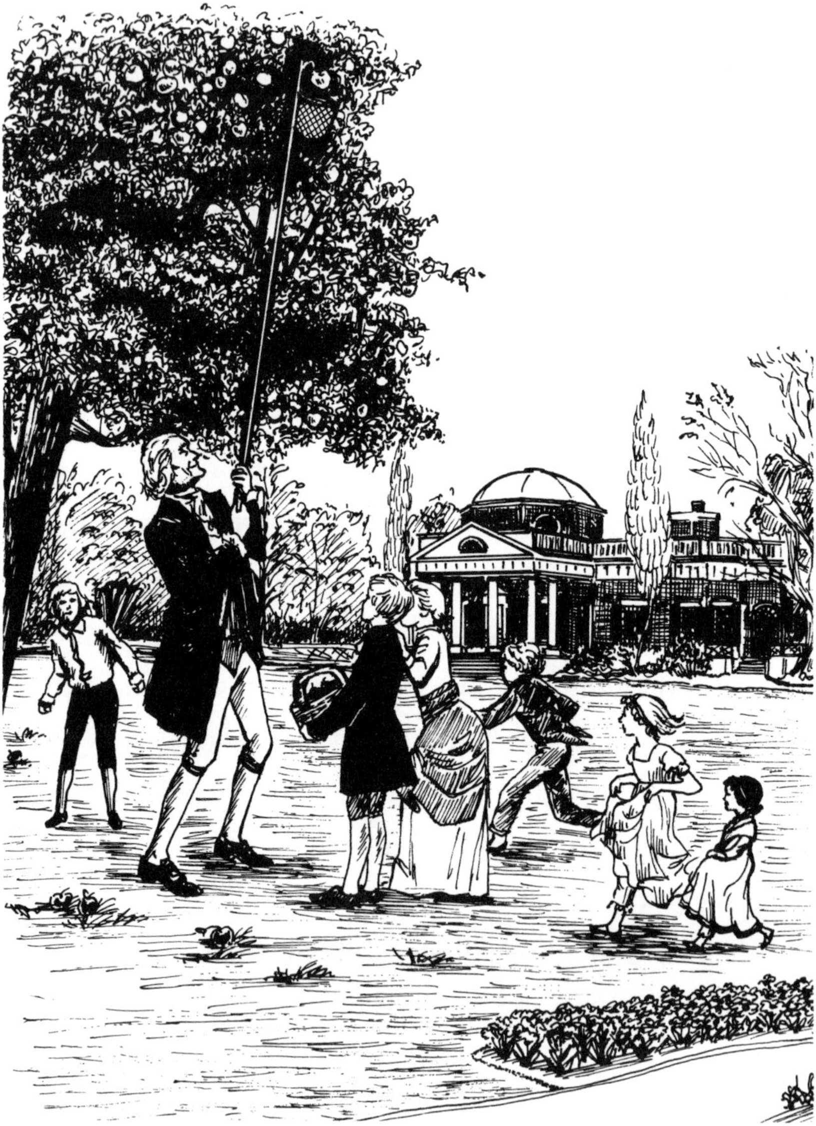

Thomas Jefferson had served as President for eight years. Like George Washington, he decided not to seek a third term. He left Washington, D.C., and went home to Monticello. There was much to do. In his absence, Monticello had not been kept in good repair.

These later years of his life were among his happiest. He spent a lot of time inventing all sorts of devices for his home. He made a clock which told the day of the week as well as the time of day. He built special desks and chairs. Farming continued to hold his main interest. He continued to experiment with the rotation of crops, fertilizers, plows and threshing machines.

Jefferson especially loved the time spent with his grandchildren. Martha and her family of eleven children lived with him. Polly's son visited often. They enjoyed simple pleasures, such as walking in the woods or gathering fruit and flowers from the gardens.

Jefferson remained popular. Many came to visit. Others wrote letters. He received about 1,000 letters a year. He tried to answer them.

Jefferson even renewed his friendship with John Adams. The two wrote often. And although Jefferson had retired from politics, he was constantly consulted on public affairs. Both James Madison and James Monroe, who followed him as President, sought his advice.

But all was not well. Jefferson was heavily in debt. Not only were there family members to support, but he also entertained lavishly.

In 1815, Jefferson sold his library of more than 6,400 books to Congress. They were to replace those that the British had destroyed during the War of 1812. The money would help. But it would not be enough.

Jefferson's friends didn't want him to lose Monticello. They collected funds on his behalf. Enough was collected to save Monticello while he was alive. Unfortunately, it was not enough to save it for his family.

Still, Jefferson's last years were fulfilling. One of his proudest achievements was the creation of the University of Virginia. It was built in Charlottesville, near Monticello. Jefferson designed some of the buildings. He liked to watch the construction through his telescope. Sometimes he would even go down the mountain to help!

But Jefferson did more than that. He planned the curriculum, hired the faculty and selected many of the library books. In March 1825 he had the joy of seeing the University of Virginia open with forty students.

When Thomas Jefferson was 83 years of age, he became quite ill. He called his family to his side. He told them farewell and gave them his final advice on how to conduct their lives. He died in his bed on July 4, 1826. It was the fiftieth anniversary of the signing of the Declaration of Independence! His friend John Adams died the same day.

Jefferson had given instructions for the inscription on his tombstone. It read:

> "Here was buried Thomas Jefferson, author of the Declaration of American Independence, of the Statute of Virginia for Religious Freedom, and Father of the University of Virginia."